Peck, Peck, Peck

Rourke
Publishing LLC
Vero Beach, Florida 32964

Molly Carroll
Kelli L. Hicks

www.rourkepublishing.com

PHOTO CREDITS: © gary718: Title Page; © Eric Isselée: page 3, 4; © Roberto Sanchez: page 5; © Amanda Rohde: page 6; © Lynn Stone: page 7, 9, 15; © inspireme: page 8; © Eva Serrabassa: page 10; © Graham Heywood: page 11; © Angelika Schwarz: page 12; © Kiyosha Takahase: page 13; © David Degan: page 14; © Marianne Guntow: page 16; © Gertjan Hooijer: page 17; © Dusty Cline: page 18 top; © Curt Pickens: page 18 bottom; © John Carnemolla: page 19; © James McQuillan: page 20; © Laura Young: page 21

Editor: Jeanne Sturm

Cover design by: Nicola Stratford: bdpublishing.com

Interior design by: Renee Brady

Library of Congress Cataloging-in-Publication Data

Hicks, Kelli L.
  Peck, peck, peck / Kelli L.Hicks.
     p. cm. -- (First science library)
  ISBN 978-1-60472-539-1
  1. Bill (Anatomy)--Juvenile literature. I. Title.
  QL697.H53 2009
  598.14'4--dc22
                              2008025162

Printed in the USA

CG/CG

Rourke Publishing

www.rourkepublishing.com – rourke@rourkepublishing.com
Post Office Box 3328, Vero Beach, FL 32964

Instead of lips, birds have beaks.

Beaks can greet

other beaks.

Beaks preen,
keeping pelicans'
feathers neat
and clean.

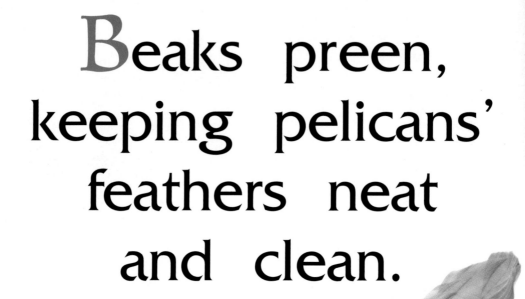

7

Beaks carry leaves
to build a nest.

Beaks fish for food to munch.

11

Beaks sip like

a straw.

Beaks are knife
and fork for
the eagle
to eat lunch.

15

Beaks peck and drill for bugs.

17

Beaks want to find

a meal of worms

 or grubs.

YUCK !

Beaks can

open seeds.

Glossary

beaks (BEEKS): Beaks are the hard, horny parts of birds' mouths. Beaks are not used to chew food. The bird swallows the food whole. Some birds use their beaks to open seeds or nuts.

eagle (EE-guhl): An eagle is a large bird of prey that often nests in the mountains. Eagles have good eyesight. Eagles have powerful, sharp claws called talons.

grubs (GRUHBZ): Grubs are the young form of some insects. They look like short, white worms. Most grubs will turn into beetles. Birds like to eat grubs.

nest (NEST): A nest is a cozy place or shelter where birds and other animals lay their eggs. Some birds make a nest out of twigs and leaves. Some birds make a burrow in the ground to keep their eggs safe.

Index

Further Reading

Collard, Sneed. *Beaks!* Charlesbridge Publishing, Inc., 2002.

Swinburne, Stephen. *Unbeatable Beaks*. Henry Holt & Company, Inc., 1999.

Gray, Samantha, Sarah Walker, and Mary Ling. *Eye Wonder: Birds (Eye Wonder)*. DK Publishing, Inc., 2002.

Websites

www.peteducation.com

www.normanbirdsanctuary.org

www.nationalzoo.si.edu/animals/birds/forkids

www.birdchannel.com/kids-bird-club

About the Authors

Kelli Hicks lives in Tampa with her husband and daughter. They enjoy sitting in the sunshine together to watch the Blue Jays and Cardinals that live in their backyard.